Social Needs

By Aaron Fields

Illustrated by: Amelia Alvin

ISBN: 978-1-953962-46-1

Parenting/Caregiver Tips

By incorporating these tips, you'll be able to meet your child's social needs and help them learn how to interact with others around them. Not only children will develop their own individuality within their community, they will also gain skills to communicate with other people and process their actions and decision makings.

When it comes to social needs, consider learning about the importance of:

- Friendship & social interaction
- Acceptance & belonging
- Opportunities for cooperation & teamwork
- Respecting or understanding diversity
- Guidance in developing social skills

Imagine a world where you have friends who make you smile and laugh, where you share toys and play games together.

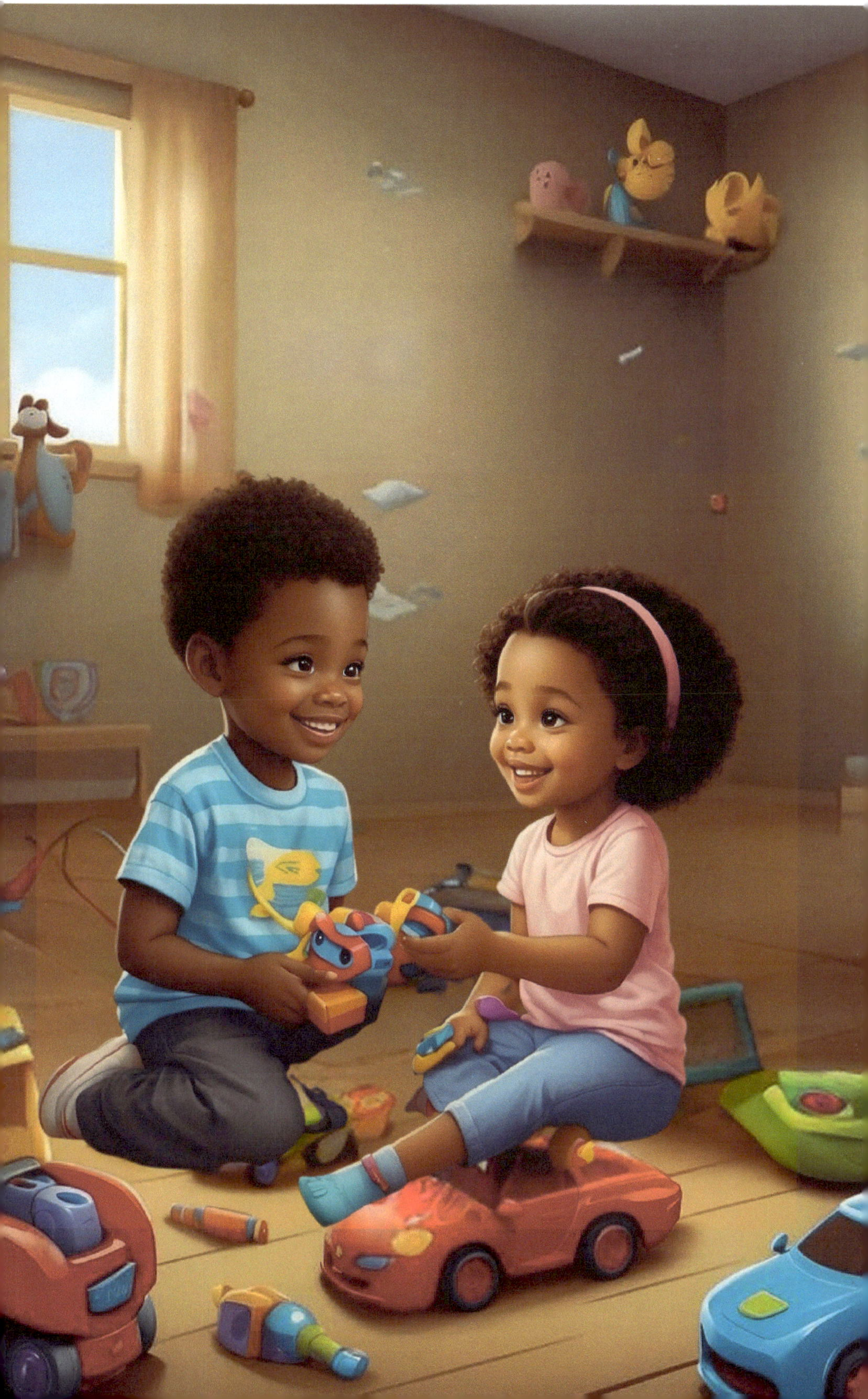

Friendship is like having a special treasure that makes your heart feel warm and happy.

Feeling accepted means knowing that you are loved and valued.

It's like being part of a big, cozy family where everyone belongs and feels safe to be themselves.

Working together with others is like putting puzzle pieces together to create something amazing.

When we cooperate and help each other, we can achieve great things and make the world a better place.

Just like a garden with flowers of all colors and shapes, our world is full of different people who bring unique perspectives and talents.

Respecting diversity means celebrating what makes each of us special and including everyone in our circle of friends that brings value.

Learning how to communicate, share, and listen to others is like learning to dance to a beautiful melody.

With guidance from caring adults and friends, children can grow into confident and kind individuals who know how to navigate the wonderful world of social interactions.

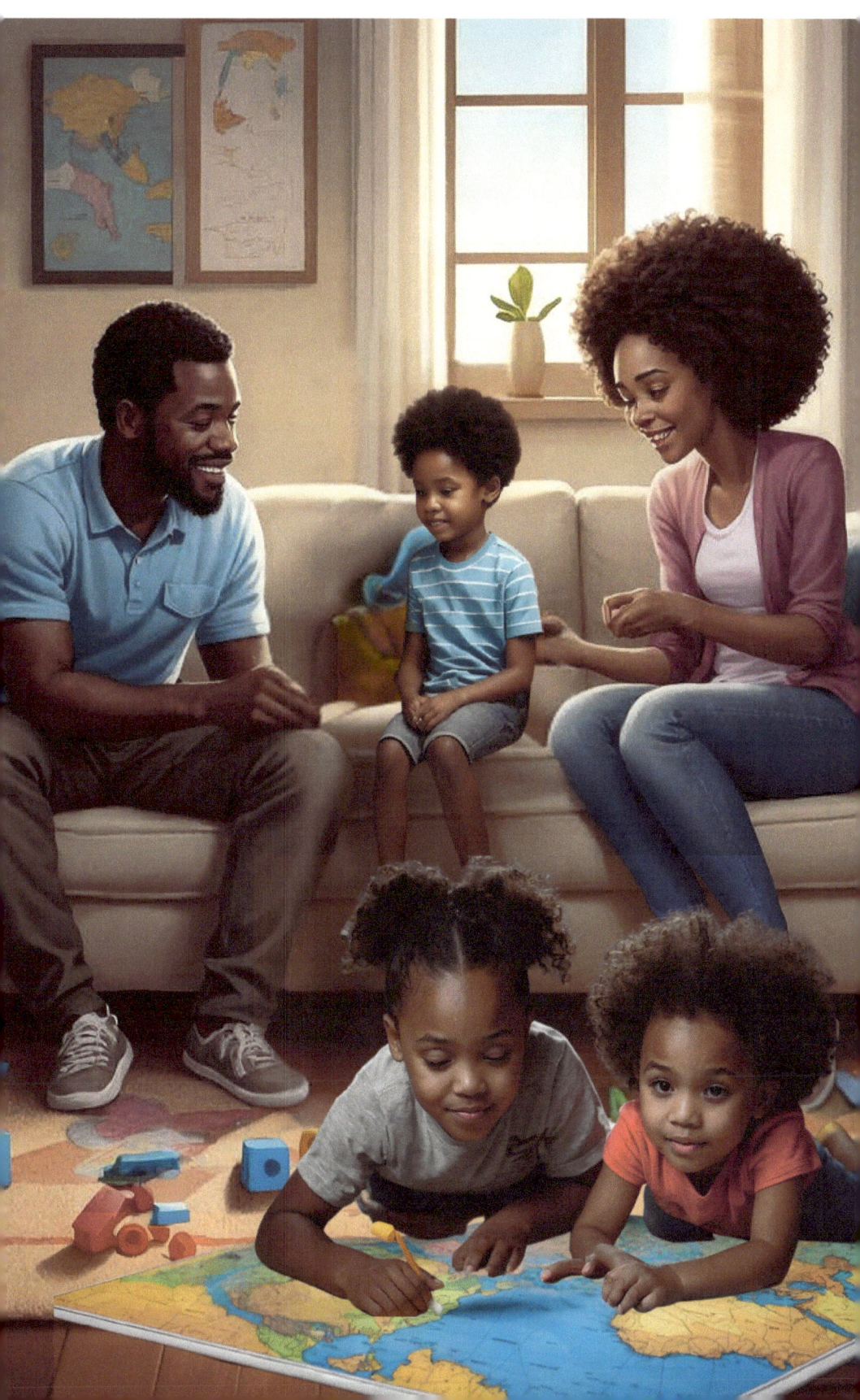

Parenting/Caregiver Tips

- Encourage your child to participate in group activities, sports or clubs where they can meet new friends and develop social skills.
- Teach children the importance of communication, empathy and active listening in building healthy relationships.
- Create a safe and supportive environment at home where your child feels loved and valued. Encourage them to embrace their unique gifts and talents.
- Engage your child in activities that require teamwork and cooperation, such as team sports or group projects.
- Teach children the value of working together towards a common goal.
- Help your child to understand that everyone is different, whether it's racial, cultural, or personal belief.
- It's important to guide and support children in helping them develop essential social skills such as conflict resolution, communication and problem-solving. Try role-playing scenarios that will help them feel more confident in social settings.

*Always remember that every child is unique. That's why it's important to tailor your approach to their individual needs. Positive reinforcement, consistent communication and leading by example are key components in fostering healthy social development in young children.

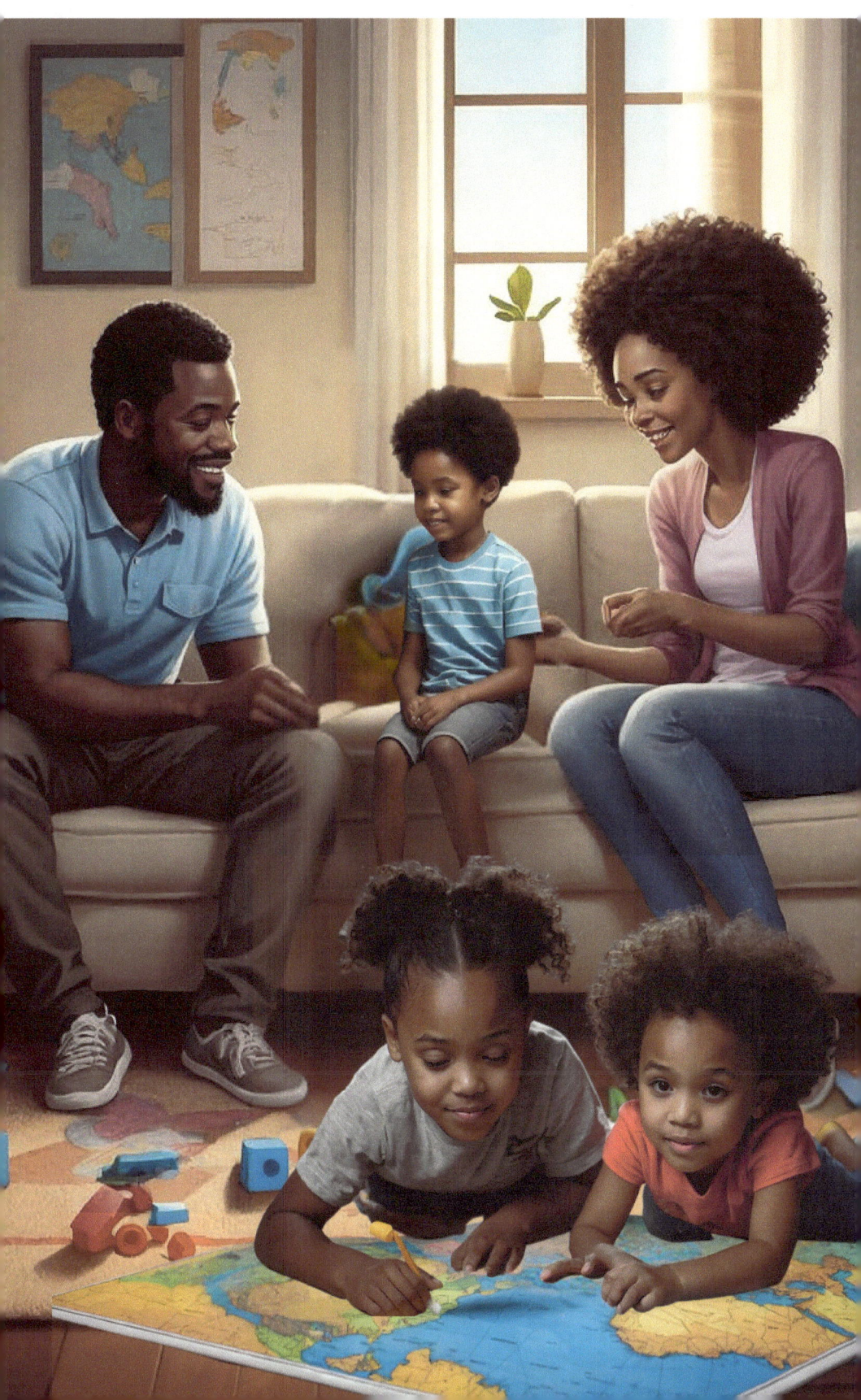

www.ingramcontent.com/pod-product-compliance
Lightning Source LLC
Chambersburg PA
CBHW040034110426
42741CB00030B/25